A MACDONALD BOOK

First published 1975
Reprinted 1977, 1978,
    1979, 1980, 1981,
    1982, 1984, 1985
Macdonald & Co
    (Publishers) Ltd
Maxwell House
Worship Street
London EC2A 2EN
A member of BPCC plc

ISBN 0 356 04889 6
(cased edition)
ISBN 0 356 06502 2
(limp edition)

Printed and bound in
Great Britain by
Purnell & Sons (Book
    Production) Ltd
Member of the
BPCC Group
Paulton, Bristol

Editor
Verity Weston

Design
Sarah Tyzack

Production
Philip Hughes

Illustrators
Peter Connolly
Peter Thornley
Peter North/The Garden
    Studio
Ron Hayward Associates
Faulkner/Marks
Tony Payne

Consultant
Harry Strongman
Senior Lecturer in History
Berkshire College of
Education

Photographs
Scala: 8
Courtesy of British Museum: 11, 54
Mansell Collection: 10, 26, 27, 55
Picturepoint: 12, 40
Sonia Halliday: 13, 16 (T, BR), 17, 19(B), 32, 33(T), 37

Pictor: 16(BL)
Colour Library International: 16(C)
C. M. Dixon: 18, 33(B), 49
Museum Calvet, Avignon: 19(T)
Ronald Grant: 30
Science Museum, London (Crown Copyright): 42

The Romans

Joan Forman

Macdonald Educational

The Romans

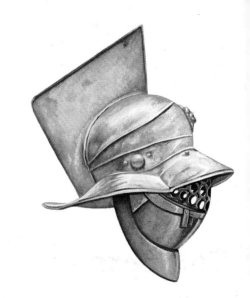

The history of Rome spans almost a thousand years. From 753 BC to 509 BC, Rome was a kingdom of small farmers. When the last king was deposed, Rome became a republic governed by important men of the city. During this time, Rome began to conquer her neighbours, until all Italy was under the rule of the Roman Republic.

In the first century BC soldier-politicians, such as Julius Caesar and Pompey, fought fierce civil wars. The Republic began to crumble. After Caesar was murdered in 44 BC, Rome found a strong leader in Caesar's nephew, Augustus. Under his leadership, the Empire began.

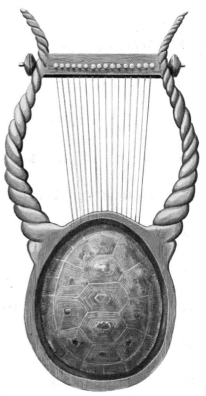

The influence of the Roman Empire spread through the whole of the then-known world and it still affects us today. The Romans took many of their ideas on architecture, religion, literature, art and politics from the Greeks, whom they greatly admired. The Romans made their own additions to the Greek ideas and spread them to the ends of the Empire.

By the time Roman power collapsed in the fifth century AD, Rome had united many peoples and lands under one government. With Greece, she had given Western civilization the foundations of law, order, art and intellectual discipline.

This book describes how the Romans lived during the years of their greatness. They have left us much evidence about their lives in their art, architecture and writings. Ruins of Roman cities such as Pompeii also form a faithful mirror of how the Romans lived.

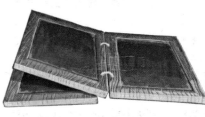

The text and illustrations in this book are all based on these sources. Together they give a picture of how it felt to be a Roman in the great days of Rome.

Contents

How Rome began

▼ This relief tells the story of Romulus and Remus. The twins are taken from their mother by her uncle, King Amulius. They are left by the river to die. A she-wolf finds the babies and feeds them.

The Romans did not really know how their city began. A legend told how Rome was founded by Romulus, a son of the war god, Mars. Romulus had a twin brother called Remus. When they were babies, they were left to die by the River Tiber. A she-wolf rescued the twins and looked after them. When the boys were grown up, they founded a city by the Tiber. Romulus killed Remus during a quarrel. Then Romulus called the city Rome, after his own name.

Historians and archaeologists believe that seven hundred years before the birth of Christ, Rome was just a collection of mud huts with thatched roofs. The huts stood on a hill near the River Tiber which was later to be called the Palatine Hill.

The climate was pleasant and the soil was fertile. The people who lived in the village on the Palatine Hill were farmers. They harvested crops of corn, olives and grapes. They kept sheep and cattle in the pasture land around their village. The farmers were called Latins and the district was called Latium.

There were six other hills nearby. As the years passed, the villages in the district grew larger. Then all the villages joined together to become one town, with seven hills within its walls. This town was to become the great city of Rome.

▼ This is an artist's recon-struction of how the hills of Rome must have looked to the first inhabitants. Modern archaeologists have found traces of these ancient huts. The nearest huts are on the Palatine Hill. The Capitol Hill is in the centre of the picture. The area between the hills is marshland, where later Romans were to build the *Forum*.

Government

▼ Julius Caesar was a brilliant man, a great general and politician. By 45 BC, he had become the sole ruler of Rome. He governed wisely, but certain Romans feared that he would make himself king. To prevent this, they stabbed him to death in the Senate House on March 15, 44 BC.

1. The first Romans were conquered by their neighbours, the Etruscans. In 509 BC, there was an Etruscan king of Rome called Tarquin the Proud. The citizens rebelled against Tarquin and drove him from the city. The Romans decided not to have any more kings and Rome became a republic.

Veto

3. Roman citizens were either rich, powerful patricians or powerless plebeians (working people). In 494 BC, the plebeians threatened to leave Rome and build their own city. After this they were allowed to elect two representatives called tribunes, who could stop any action of the Senate by calling "Veto!" (I forbid).

2. When Rome became a republic, the power of the king was shared between two men, called consuls. The consuls held office for one year. A citizens' Assembly and a council, called the Senate, helped the consuls to govern. The Senate was responsible for finance and foreign policy. The Assembly made the city's laws.

▼ After Caesar's death, his nephew, Octavian (below), and his friend, Mark Antony, ruled the state. The two men quarrelled when Antony left his wife (who was Octavian's sister) for Queen Cleopatra of Egypt. Antony was defeated in battle in 31 BC, and Octavian became the first Roman Emperor.

4. As the Roman Empire grew, the rich became richer and the poor became more discontented. There were riots and civil wars. Successful generals fought one another as well as fighting the enemies of Rome. Peace came in 31 BC, when Octavian became Augustus, the first Roman Emperor.

A great empire

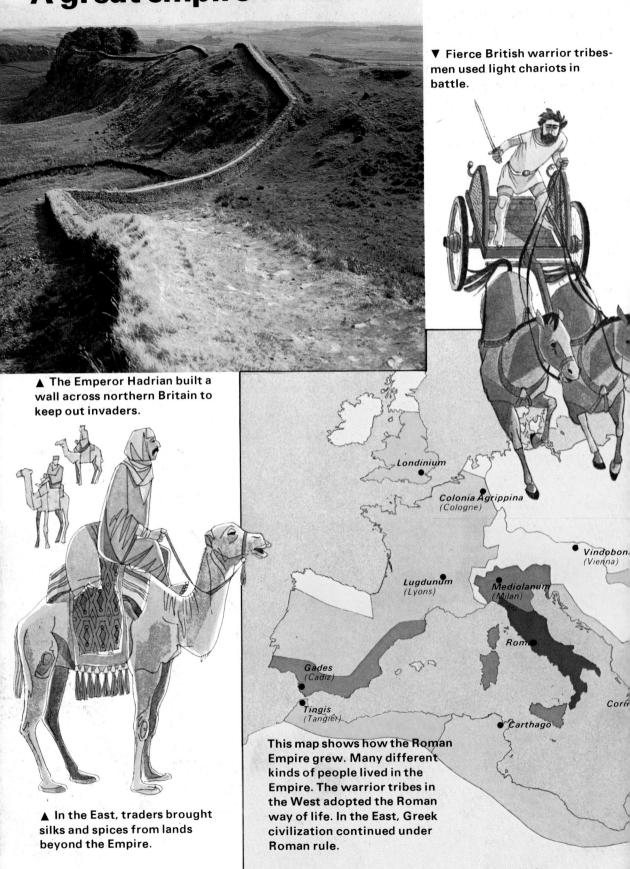

▼ Fierce British warrior tribes-men used light chariots in battle.

▲ The Emperor Hadrian built a wall across northern Britain to keep out invaders.

Londinium

Colonia Agrippina
(Cologne)

Vindobon
(Vienna)

Lugdunum
(Lyons)

Mediolanum
(Milan)

Rom

Gades
(Cadiz)

Tingis
(Tangier)

Carthago

Cori

▲ In the East, traders brought silks and spices from lands beyond the Empire.

This map shows how the Roman Empire grew. Many different kinds of people lived in the Empire. The warrior tribes in the West adopted the Roman way of life. In the East, Greek civilization continued under Roman rule.

The first inhabitants of the Roman Republic only fought to protect their lands from invaders. The main enemies of early Rome were the neighbouring Etruscan states. One by one, Rome defeated the Etruscan armies. By 264 BC, Rome ruled most of the Italian peninsula.

In 264 BC, the great trading and seafaring republic of Carthage controlled the Mediterranean. During the next 120 years, Rome fought three great wars against Carthage. The fighting was very bitter. By 140 BC, the city of Carthage had been totally destroyed and her provinces in Spain and Sicily were under Roman rule.

By 121 BC, most of the lands around the Mediterranean had either been conquered or become allies of Rome.

In the first century BC, Julius Caesar conquered the warrior tribes of Gaul and his rival, Pompey, conquered Syria and Palestine. When Queen Cleopatra committed suicide in 31 BC, Octavian made Egypt a Roman province. Southern Britain was added to the Empire in AD 43.

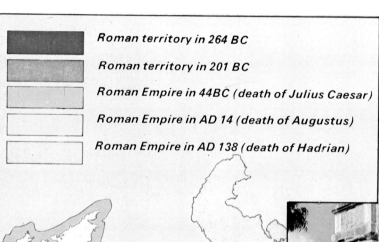

Roman territory in 264 BC

Roman territory in 201 BC

Roman Empire in 44BC (death of Julius Caesar)

Roman Empire in AD 14 (death of Augustus)

Roman Empire in AD 138 (death of Hadrian)

Byzantium

Antiochia

Alexandria

▲ This Greek philosopher could have taught in Rome. The Romans copied Greek ideas and learned Greek as a second language.

▼ Many Roman buildings, such as this triumphal arch at Sbeitla in Tunisia, can still be seen today.

A rich man's villa

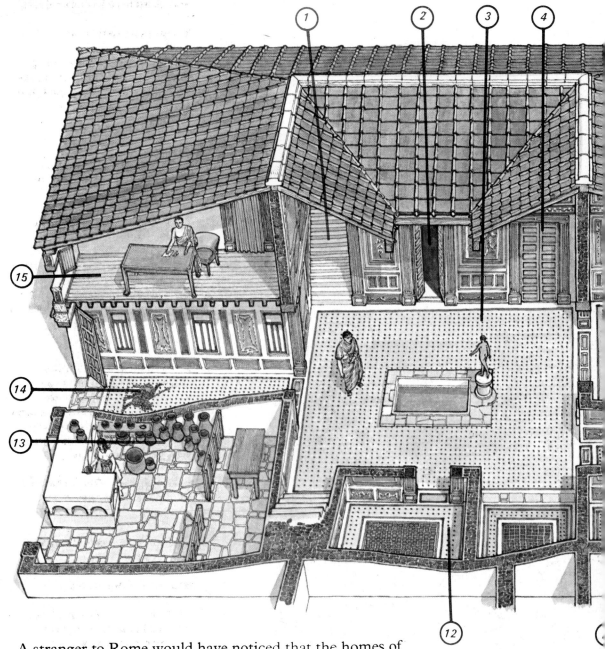

A stranger to Rome would have noticed that the homes of rich people were very different from the homes of poor people. The rich lived in mansions where there were marble columns, floors and walls. Rich people owned luxurious curtains, and furniture made of bronze or ivory or rare and expensive wood.

Wealthy people paid skilled artists to decorate their villas. The artists painted lovely frescoes on the walls. They decorated the floors with mosaic patterns. Even the wealthy, however, had no glass for their windows and few kitchens had fireplaces or chimneys.

▲ This is an artist's reconstruction of a villa at Pompeii with part of the upstairs and roof cut away. We have learned much about the way people lived in ancient Rome from the excavations at Pompeii and Herculaneum. These two towns were buried in ash and cinder during an eruption of the volcano, Vesuvius, in AD 79.

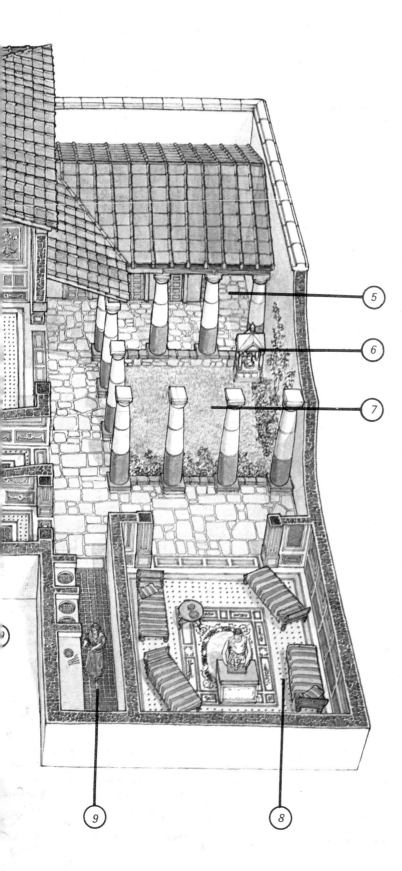

1. Stairs leading to a bedroom. Bedrooms were usually small and contained little furniture.

2. Door to a bedroom.

3. The *atrium* or main living room. This room had an opening in the roof and a small pool in the floor beneath it.

4. Door to a bedroom.

5. The peristyle. This was a covered passage around an open courtyard.

6. The *lararium,* the shrine of the household gods.

7. The courtyard of the peristyle, bordered by flower-beds and shrubs. Archaeologists found seeds from some of the original plants when they were excavating Pompeii.

8. The *triclinium* or dining room. The *triclinium* was usually small. It contained three or four couches on which the diners would lie, leaving very little room for the slaves who waited on them.

9. The kitchen. The fuel burned in the ovens was wood or charcoal.

10. The *tablinium,* a reception room or study.

11 and 12. Bedrooms.

13. A shop. The owner of the villa let his spare rooms to shopkeepers. There was another shop on the other side of the entrance passage.

14. In the entrance passage there was a mosaic sign on the floor, *Cave Canem,* which means Beware of the Dog.

15. An upper room, which would probably have been let as a shop. There would have been a separate entrance from the street.

Houses and slums

The poor people of Rome lived in small rooms over shops or in tenement blocks, which were rather like modern blocks of flats. A single tenement block was so large that it looked like an "island" in the surrounding streets and was called an *insula*.

Poor homes only contained one or two uncomfortable beds and a stool or chair. Most women owned a spindle for spinning thread and a weaving frame for making cloth. In the winter, most homes were heated by a charcoal fire burning in a brazier. If the fire went out it was very difficult to light again.

▲ The peristyle of a villa at Pompeii.

◀ A view of part of Pompeii as it is today.

▼ At Bulla Regia in Tunisia, the Romans built underground villas. This is the dining room in one of them.

▲ The courtyard of a villa at Herculaneum.

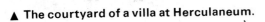

When Octavian became Emperor, there were more than 45,000 tenement blocks in Rome. There was little room for building in the city. The *insulae* were tall and narrow. They usually had at least five storeys.

The builders often used cheap, poor-quality materials. The *insulae* were sometimes so badly constructed that the walls cracked or the roofs fell in. Cicero, who was a wealthy landlord, complained, "Two of my buildings have collapsed, and in the others the walls are all cracked. Not only the tenants, but even the mice have left."

There was no water supply on the upper floors of the *insulae*, so there was no plumbing or central heating. The tenants used public lavatories or they poured their slops from the windows after dark. There was always a danger of fire and houses often burned down.

The Romans liked gardens, but poor people had no space for them and had to be content with window boxes.

▲ Archaeologists found this multi-seater public lavatory at Dougga, in Tunisia.

▼ A Roman slum. There is a tavern on the left with a wine-jar sign on the wall outside.

Home and school

▶ A newborn baby was bathed by the midwife in a large basin. A baby was not accepted into the family until it had been seen by the father.

▲ Children at school wrote on wax tablets with a bone stylus.

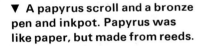

▼ A papyrus scroll and a bronze pen and inkpot. Papyrus was like paper, but made from reeds.

The citizens of Rome enjoyed social life. The rich entertained a great deal. Both rich and poor spent much of their time out of doors during the day, attending the Games or visiting the public baths. It was dangerous to wander in the Roman streets at night, so most people returned home before sunset.

A Roman father had complete power over his children and over his wife. Boys were expected to obey their fathers, even when they were grown up. In later times, wives gained some independence from their husbands when they were allowed to have property of their own.

Rich people's children went to school. The school might be just one room, or a booth separated from the street by only a curtain. The teachers were usually Greeks, who might also be slaves. Many teachers were harsh and often beat their pupils. Boys and girls went to different elementary schools where they learned reading, writing and arithmetic.

When girls were 13, they left school. They continued their education at home, where they were trained to be good housewives. Boys went on to secondary school when they were 13. As well as going to school, boys were prepared for a life in the army. They were taught how to fight and they learned to endure hardship.

▼ Many Romans enjoyed a happy family life. They made a record of their happiness in carvings, such as this one.

▶ A modern reconstruction of a Roman lyre. Girls were taught to sing and to play the lyre as part of their education.

▶ A mosaic of a child's goose cart. Toy carts were also pulled by dogs.

▼ Dice were made of marble or bone. Each side of the knuckle bones on the right had a different score. The counters below were also used in games. *Nugator* meant "trifler".

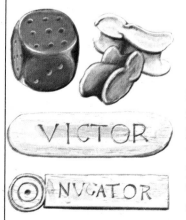

School started early in the morning and finished in the middle of the afternoon. After school, pupils might go to the public baths or play games. Popular children's games were "blindman's buff", "nuts" or "king". Children also played with hoops, toys and dolls. They enjoyed dressing up. Sometimes they wore frightening masks. They played at being judges, kings and gladiators.

A nobleman's life

1. Roman babies were named when a few days old. Boys had three names: a first name such as Marcus; a second, which was that of his clan (perhaps Julius or Flavius) and a third family name (Cicero, Caesar). Each baby was given a lucky charm called a *bulla.*

2. At elementary school, a boy learned reading, writing and arithmetic. When he was 13, he went to secondary school where his teacher was a Greek *grammaticus.* A boy might finally go on to a *rhetor's* school where he learned the art of eloquence, or rhetoric.

5. At 39, a Roman noble could be elected as a *praetor.* There were eight *praetors.* They either presided over the law courts or they became provincial governors. During his year in office, a *praetor* was responsible for publishing the laws of the state.

6. An ex-*praetor* could become a consul at 42. During the Republic, the two consuls were very powerful. They presided over the Senate and commanded the army. After the first century BC, consuls had less power although they were still respected officials.

3. Marriages were usually arranged by parents. The bride might be only 13 and her bridegroom a little older. After the wedding there was a banquet, then a torchlight procession to the bridegroom's house, where the bride was carried over the threshold.

4. At 30, an ambitious man might be elected as a *quaestor*. A *quaestor* worked in the treasury or as assistant to a provincial governor. A successful *quaestor* was elected as an aedile. The aedile supervised the city's food supply, traffic and entertainment.

7. Consuls spent only a year in office. An ex-consul could become a pro-consul. A pro-consul might govern an important province where he could become very rich. Many pro-consuls made enough money to keep them in luxury for the rest of their lives.

8. When a noble Roman died, he was dressed in his official robes and crowned with laurel leaves. Then his body was carried on a bier to the funeral. This was announced by a public crier. Relatives gathered to hear the funeral speeches before the body was burned.

Clothes and fashions

Most Romans wore a piece of cloth shaped like a blanket and called a toga. The toga could be square or oblong and was draped on the body in folds. Togas were made of wool until Rome began trading with Egypt. Then Romans started wearing clothes made of Egyptian linen.

Men wore white togas. Senators wore togas with a broad purple stripe. Small boys had a narrow purple stripe on their togas. Women varied the colour of their clothes by using vegetable dyes. Rich women liked to wear perfume, cosmetics and jewelry. Roman men and women wore wigs and even false teeth when they had lost their own.

Three slaves help their mistress to dress and put on her make-up. Each woman wears a full length tunic called a *stola*.

The slave wears a simple tunic. The master wears a loosely-draped garment called a toga over his tunic.

Hairstyles

Fashions in hairstyles changed as often as they do today. Both sexes curled their hair with curling tongs to create elaborate hair-styles. Men and women put oil and grease on their heads to make their hair grow.

Beauty aids

Bronze and tin mirror with silver gilt border

Ivory cosmetics pot

Onyx scent bottle

Ivory comb with owner's name on it

MODESTINAVHEE

Silver spatulas for applying cosmetics

Going to the baths

The public baths were a source of great pleasure to the Romans. Citizens could spend the whole day there. The buildings were luxurious and provided all kinds of amusements. As well as baths, there were gymnasiums, gardens, shops and libraries.

The Baths of Caracalla in Rome covered 13 hectares (33 acres) and had a stadium as well as room for 1600 bathers. There were three or four different kinds of bathing, from the very cold to the very hot. A bather could take his choice. All baths were very noisy places. Romans liked to sing and whistle as well as gossip.

Library

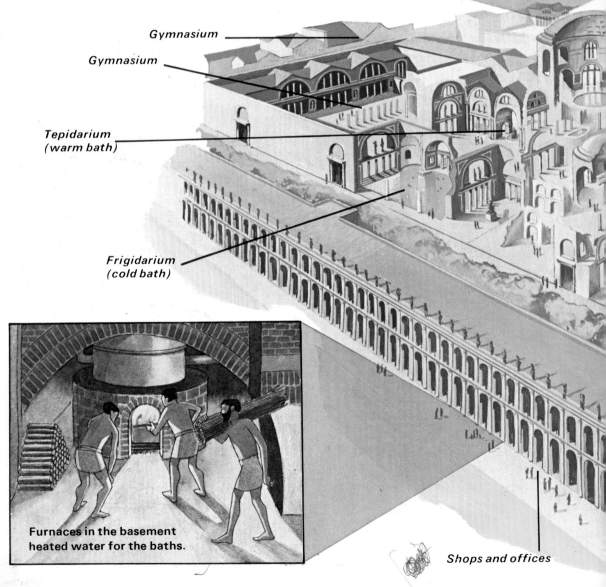

Gymnasium

Gymnasium

Tepidarium
(warm bath)

Frigidarium
(cold bath)

Furnaces in the basement heated water for the baths.

Shops and offices

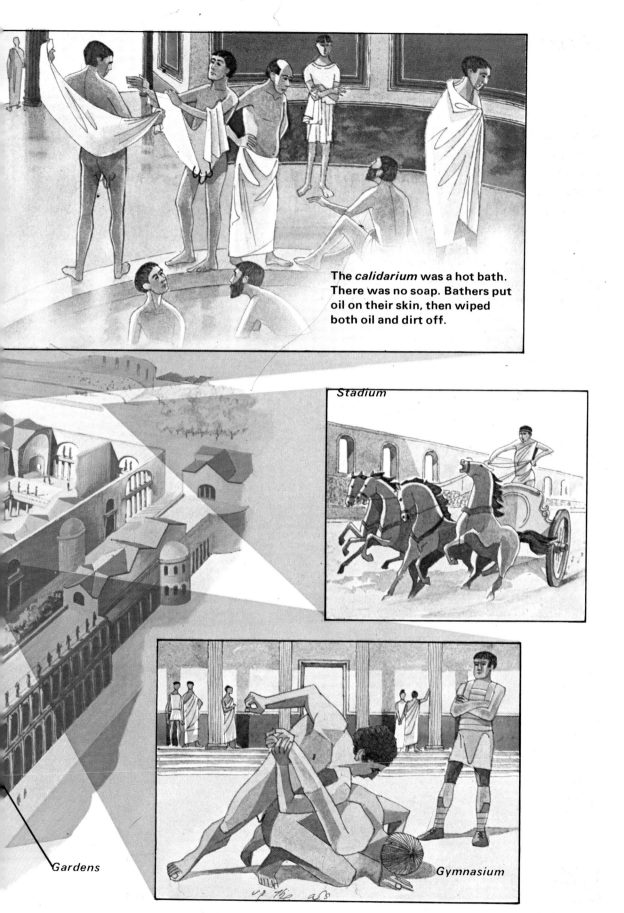

The *calidarium* was a hot bath. There was no soap. Bathers put oil on their skin, then wiped both oil and dirt off.

Stadium

Gardens

Gymnasium

Shopping in Rome

▲ A butcher. We know much about everyday life from carvings like these on Roman tombs.

▼ A poultry shop.

Shops in Rome opened early in the morning and closed at midday. They opened again later in the day and stayed open until dusk. Trade was carried on in the street as well as inside the shops.

There were barbers, booksellers, grocers, bakers, poultry-sellers, furniture shops and stalls selling cooked meats. There were a few money-lenders' shops, but wealthy Romans looked down on this occupation. Cato wrote "There is more to be made in money-lending, but no gentleman would be a money-lender". Most shopkeepers were slaves or ex-slaves. Romans had a poor opinion of shopkeepers. They thought that shopkeepers would even sell themselves for the right price.

One of the most flourishing trades was that of selling oil. Oil was used for lamps and cooking. It was also used instead of soap for washing. Large quantities of oil changed hands each day. By AD 300, there were 2,300 oil-sellers in Rome.

Excavations at Pompeii show that merchants' shops were often built next to their private houses. One merchant had a sign over his villa which said "Hail, Profit".

▲ A draper shows cloth to buyers.

▲ A goldsmith at work. You can see part of the scales which hung above him.

▲ This pharmacist made medicines in her shop, helped by a servant.

Bread, porridge and banquets

▲ A bronze egg pan, saucepan and ladle.

Ordinary Romans ate little meat. The main food for most people was wheat flour, which they made into bread or porridge. Roman cooks added herbs, olives, vegetables and other flavourings to their porridge to make it more interesting.

Romans got up at sunrise and finished work at about three in the afternoon. They arranged their meals to fit in with the working day. For breakfast, school children ate a wheat pancake biscuit with salt, dates, honey or olives. Adults might dip this in wine. At midday, the ordinary family ate a main dish of savoury wheatmeal porridge.

Wealthy people had a larger menu to choose from and they ate much more meat than the poor. At a dinner party people might eat up to seven courses. A small army of slaves looked after the rich while they ate. One or two slaves were always on duty with peacock feather fans to keep the flies off the food.

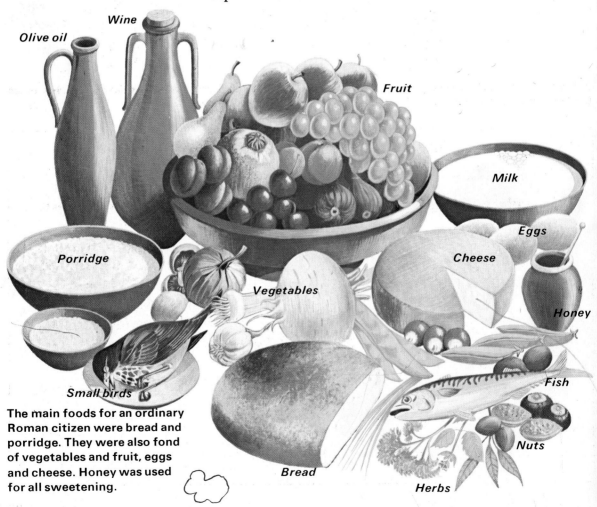

Olive oil

Wine

Fruit

Milk

Eggs

Porridge

Cheese

Vegetables

Honey

Small birds

Fish

The main foods for an ordinary Roman citizen were bread and porridge. They were also fond of vegetables and fruit, eggs and cheese. Honey was used for all sweetening.

Nuts

Bread

Herbs

▲ Food was brought into the city at night in noisy wooden-wheeled carts.

▲ Soldiers in camp ground their own corn. There was one hand-mill for every ten men.

▲ Romans who did not have an oven could take their meals to the public bakery.

▲ Rich Romans often ate and drank too much at banquets.

MENU FOR A ROMAN BANQUET

Appetizers

Jellyfish and Eggs

Sows' Udders
stuffed with salted sea urchins

Patina of Brains
cooked with milk and eggs

Boiled Tree Fungi
with peppered fish-fat sauce

Sea Urchins
with spices, honey, oil and egg sauce

Main Dishes

Fallow Deer
roasted with onion sauce, rue, Jericho dates, raisins, oil and honey

Boiled Ostrich
with a sweet sauce

Dormice
stuffed with pork and pine kernels

Ham
boiled with figs and baked in pastry with honey

Flamingo
boiled with dates

Dessert

Fricassee of Roses
with pastry

Stoned Dates
stuffed with nuts and pine kernels fried in honey

Hot African Sweet-wine Cakes
with honey

Fruit

Charioteers and gladiators

Chariot races

Athletic games such as the Greek Olympics were not very popular in Rome. The Romans preferred another kind of sport. This was the chariot race. The Romans were as enthusiastic about chariot racing as people today are about soccer. There were four regular teams in the chariot race: the Whites, the Greens, the Blues and the Reds. The Roman audience gambled heavily on which team would win each race.

Like modern pop singers, charioteers could earn enormous sums of money. The Roman people adored them and treated them as heroes. Some famous charioteers could boast of more than a thousand victories, but others were killed after only a few races.

Gladiators

A more terrible form of "entertainment" took place in the amphitheatre. It was here that gladiators, or men and wild animals, fought to the death in front of large audiences. Criminals, prisoners and later, Christians, were put into the arena to face lions and tigers that had been kept hungry for the occasion.

These displays were the favourite shows of the Roman people for several centuries. The mob in the amphitheatre had no pity for a wounded gladiator. If he was wounded in a fight, he was killed. A wounded gladiator was not thought to be of any use to anyone.

The largest amphitheatre in the Roman world was the Colosseum. The opening of the Colosseum in AD 80, was celebrated with a hundred days of continuous games.

▲ The chariot race scene from the film *Ben Hur*. Chariots could be pulled by four horses or two. The chariot was very light and was only kept steady by the charioteer's weight. It overturned easily. If this happened, the charioteer might be dragged along after the horses for the rest of the race and he would be lucky to survive.

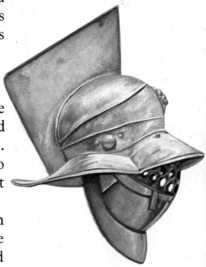

▲ This gladiator's helmet was more for decoration than protection. The wearer could see very little through the visor.

▲ To make a fight more interesting for the spectators, each
gladiator fought with different
weapons.

The Colosseum

▲ The Colosseum as it is today.

1. Catwalk round the top of the outer wall, along which archers were stationed.

2. Exits and *vomitoria*.

3. The sunblind or *velarium*.

4. Wooden pillars to support the sunshade.

5. Stone supports for the wooden pillars.

6. The Emperor's box.

7. Entrances for animals.

8. *Podium*, on which important people could walk around.

9. Large entrance for gladiators.

10. Statues of the gods in niches.

11. Marble facing on the outer walls.

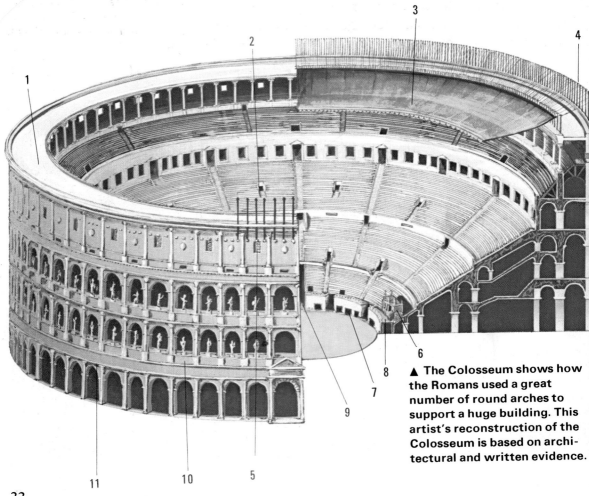

▲ The Colosseum shows how the Romans used a great number of round arches to support a huge building. This artist's reconstruction of the Colosseum is based on architectural and written evidence.

The Emperor Vespasian started to build the Colosseum. But it was not completely finished until the time of his sons, Titus and Domitian.

The Colosseum is an example of the great skill of Roman architects. It was built on the site of a lake which had belonged to the Emperor Nero. The architect's first problem was to free the site from water. He built a drainage system of stone sewers which drained the lake into the Tiber and then kept the site dry.

The Colosseum was designed to hold about 55,000 people. The crowds at the games were likely to be unruly and difficult to control: another of the architect's problems was therefore how to empty the arena quickly and safely after the show ended. He constructed 80 *vomitoria* which were great staircase exits. A full audience could leave the building by these in about three minutes.

The audience sat in rows from the arena to the high rim of the outer wall. This was 91 metres (300 feet) above the Emperor's *podium*. A catwalk ran round the top of the building, on which archers were stationed, ready to shoot any beast which escaped.

Marble, tufa and concrete were used to build the Colosseum. It was decorated magnificently. There were gilded corridors, painted ceilings and walls whose mosaics were made of precious stones.

▲ A Roman mosaic showing two men with a rhinoceros which they have caught to send to Rome. Huge numbers of wild animals were captured and killed for the Roman games.

▼ This mosaic, discovered in Tunisia, shows two gladiators killing a leopard. Battles were staged between different kinds of animals and between animals and men.

Building the aqueducts

After the Romans found good limestone near the city, their building projects became more ambitious. Engineers designed large aqueducts to carry fresh water to Rome.

Two of the most important aqueducts were the *Aqua Claudia* and the *Aqua Marcia*. The *Aqua Claudia* was 69 km. (43 miles) long. The water ran through underground channels in the hills for 55 km. (34 miles). Then it came out of the hillside to be carried in pipes on top of large arches to the city.

Huge numbers of workmen were needed to carry out Rome's great building projects. This work force was almost entirely made up of slaves who had been captured or conquered in one of Rome's many wars. Some of these men were well-educated. They became important men in the building operations. These slaves were also responsible for repairing damaged aqueducts and for putting in the pipes that carried water to private houses.

The builders used cranes and pulleys to raise the large blocks of stone into position. They employed gangs of slaves to quarry the stone and operate the building machinery. Roman engineers learned how to use both cranes and pulleys from the Greeks.

▼ This is an artist's reconstruction of the *Aqua Claudia* and the *Aqua Marcia*. Gangs of slaves are still at work on the *Aqua Claudia*. The *Aqua Marcia* loops around under the *Aqua Claudia*. The city of Rome can be seen on the horizon.

The city of Rome

The Emperor was usually responsible for large building projects. Emperors who built aqueducts and amphitheatres were sure to be popular with the citizens of Rome.

Roman builders used stone, brick, marble, granite and wood. These materials were transported on barges along the River Tiber to Rome. Roman builders invented concrete, which was a mixture of rubble and water. Building projects were regularly undertaken, particularly after a period of destruction such as the great fire in the reign of the Emperor Nero.

Many fine buildings were built near the *Forum*. The *Forum* was the main business centre of the city. Here there were shops, market squares and meeting places.

Emperors often erected buildings as memorials to their own greatness. Many of these buildings have survived. Vespasian built the Colosseum. Trajan built a column with a statue of himself on the top. Both Julius Caesar and Augustus built a forum. Augustus also built theatres, baths, libraries, temples and granaries. Augustus said, "I found a city of brick and left it marble".

The *Forum Romanum* as it appears today. The Colosseum and the Arch of Titus are in the background. The Temple of Vesta is on the left.

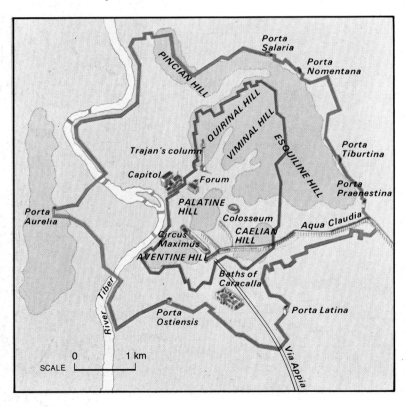

▲ A plan of Rome showing some important buildings. An early wall is shown in purple, a later wall in brown.

A country estate

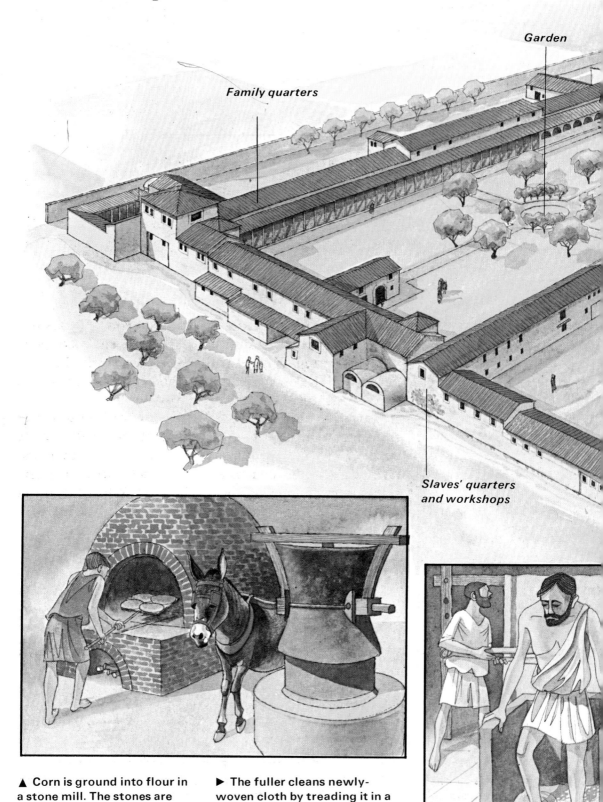

Garden

Family quarters

Slaves' quarters
and workshops

▲ Corn is ground into flour in a stone mill. The stones are turned by a donkey. The flour is made into bread and cooked in a brick oven.

▶ The fuller cleans newly-woven cloth by treading it in a tub of fuller's earth. His assistant trims the surface of the cloth to make it smooth.

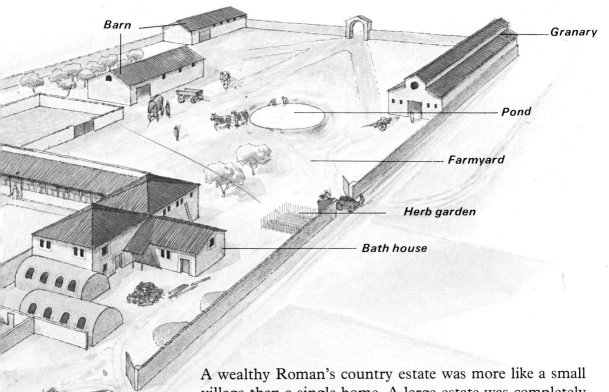

Barn

Granary

Pond

Farmyard

Herb garden

Bath house

Kitchen garden

A wealthy Roman's country estate was more like a small village than a single home. A large estate was completely self-supporting. The estate farm supplied all the food needed by the owner and the estate workers. The estate had its own vineyards and olive groves.

As well as farm buildings, there were workshops where skilled craftsmen made everything that was needed on the estate. This included food, clothes, tools, harness and farm carts. The owner employed both free men and slaves as craftsmen and farm labourers. When the owner was away the estate was run by a bailiff (*villicus*) and his wife (*villica*).

▲ Every large estate had its own blacksmith who made all the iron tools. In the background the smith's apprentice keeps the forge hot.

▲ The estate carpenter saws a plank with a bow saw. Paintings of a Roman carpenter's tools can be seen today in frescoes at Pompeii.

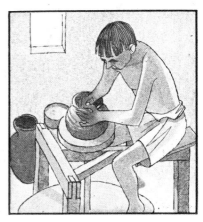

▲ Most containers for cooking and serving food were made of earthenware pottery. A large estate would usually have its own potter.

Roads and travel

As the Roman Empire grew, the Romans built a vast network of roads. The first great Roman roads, such as the *Via Appia*, joined Rome to other parts of Italy. As Roman soldiers conquered lands outside Italy, they built more roads. The roads helped them to travel safely and quickly throughout their newly-conquered lands.

Soldiers were not the only people who had to travel to distant parts of the Empire. Government officials had to go to govern the new provinces. Merchants went there to buy food and goods and take them back to Rome. So, although the roads were built first for the army, officials and merchants soon travelled on them as well.

Cross-section of a Roman road

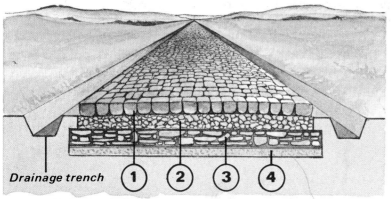

Drainage trench ① ② ③ ④

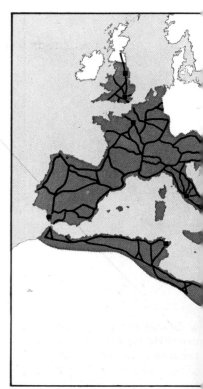

▲ A Roman road that can still be seen in Yorkshire, England.

1. The surface was made of blocks of stone in concrete.

2. Concrete, made of gravel or coarse sand mixed with lime.

3. Lime concrete mixed with broken stone.

4. Lime mortar or sand laid to form a level base.

If you had journeyed on foot along one of the main Roman roads, you might have been passed by carriages, chariots, tradesmen's carts and processions of servants travelling with their wealthy masters. You would also have been in the company of poorer people who would be travelling on foot or riding mules.

The roads would be busy near to the towns. Further away from the towns, there would be much less traffic. People avoided travelling at night because of the risk of robbers. There were inns on the roads, but they were often the haunts of thieves. Ordinary travellers did not usually spend the night at an inn. They either stayed with friends or slept in their carriages.

▼ Farm carts had solid wooden wheels. They were usually drawn by oxen.

▼ The Romans built a network of roads covering the Empire.

Roman roads

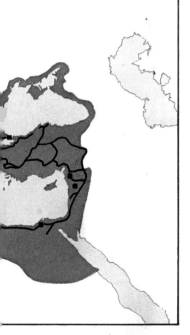

▼ People going on long journeys travelled in a covered carriage, drawn by mules.

▼ Light chariots were used for racing.

Shipping and trade

With a million people living in Rome, it was impossible to produce all their food on the nearby farms.

By the time of Julius Caesar, goods were being imported from abroad. Large cargoes were shipped into the port of Ostia. There the goods were loaded onto barges which travelled up the River Tiber to Rome. Merchant ships arrived at Ostia daily from all parts of the Empire. Merchant ships even travelled to India and back although the journey took a year.

Traders also used the great road system of the Empire. They took not only goods, but information about new methods of manufacture, from one end of the Empire to another.

▼ Roman merchant ships were built broad and deep to carry large grain cargoes. Oars were used only when the ship was becalmed.

This map shows the goods that were produced in and around the Roman Empire. Raw materials such as metals and hides came from the North. Foodstuffs came from the South.

Silks from China

Perfumes from Arabia

PRODUCE OF THE EMPIRE

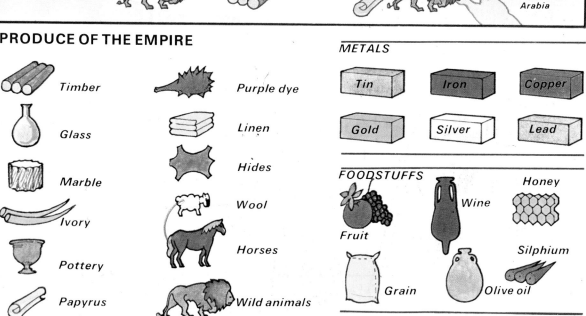

Timber

Glass

Marble

Ivory

Pottery

Papyrus

Purple dye

Linen

Hides

Wool

Horses

Wild animals

METALS

Tin

Iron

Copper

Gold

Silver

Lead

FOODSTUFFS

Fruit

Wine

Honey

Grain

Olive oil

Silphium

A soldier's life

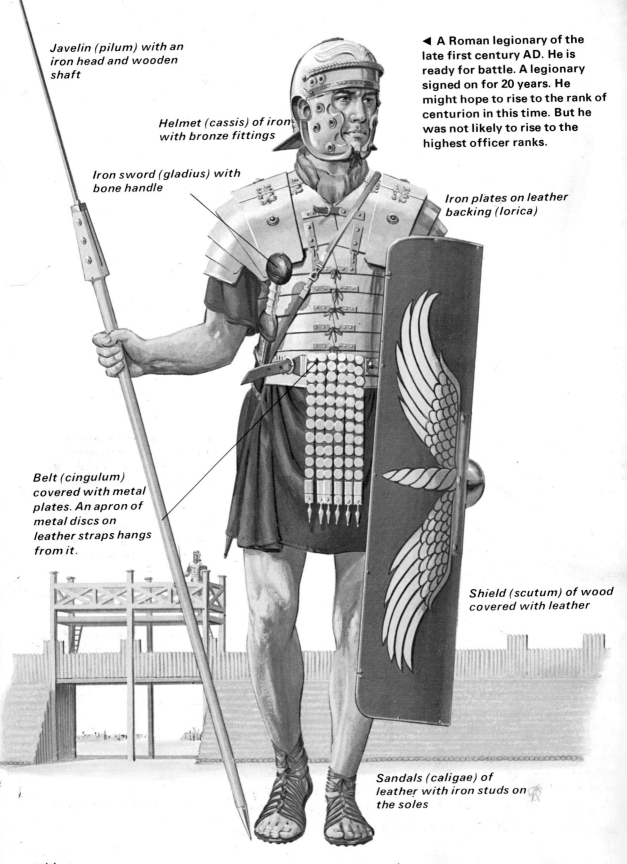

Javelin (pilum) with an iron head and wooden shaft

Helmet (cassis) of iron with bronze fittings

Iron sword (gladius) with bone handle

Belt (cingulum) covered with metal plates. An apron of metal discs on leather straps hangs from it.

◄ A Roman legionary of the late first century AD. He is ready for battle. A legionary signed on for 20 years. He might hope to rise to the rank of centurion in this time. But he was not likely to rise to the highest officer ranks.

Iron plates on leather backing (lorica)

Shield (scutum) of wood covered with leather

Sandals (caligae) of leather with iron studs on the soles

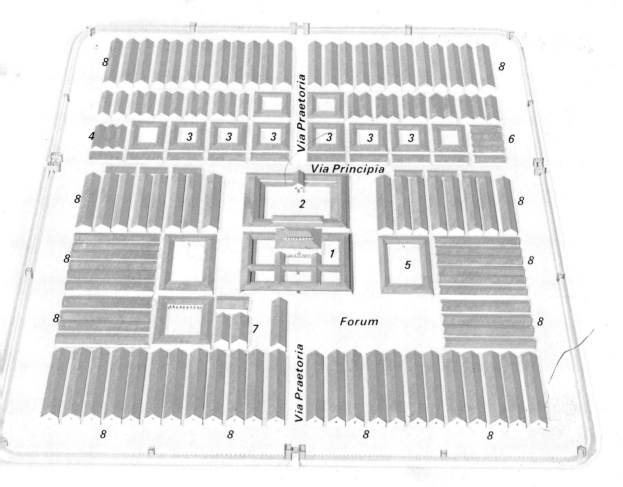

The buildings in the illustration are labelled:

4 3 3 3 *Via Praetoria* 3 3 3 6

Via Principia

2   1   5

7   Forum

Via Praetoria

8 (appears at multiple positions around the barracks)

The Roman Empire depended on a strong and efficient army to fight campaigns and protect the frontiers. Roman boys were taught to fight from childhood, so there were always men ready for the army when they were needed.

Most of the soldiers at the time of the Empire were volunteers. They joined the army because they wanted to, not because they had to. To be a legionary, you had to be a Roman citizen and you had to be at least 1.74 metres (5ft. 8in.) tall. Once a man had been accepted as a legionary, he was sent to a camp. There he was trained in marching, riding, swimming, and fighting.

In wartime, a soldier's life was a mixture of camping, long marches, terrible battles, and looting. As well as fighting, the soldiers had to build camps and bridges, put up fortifications, build or repair roads, or even sow fields with seed that they had brought from home.

When on the march, a legionary would have to walk about 29 km. (18 miles) or more a day. He had to carry enough grain for about 15 days, a basket, a pick, an axe, a saw, a cooking pot, two stakes for the camp's palisade, and his armour and weapons. Hundreds of mules carried the army's tents, extra armour and siege weapons.

▲ When legionaries were stationed in a place permanently, they lived in a fortress like this. The buildings were of stone.

1. *Praetorium,* or *domus legati* (house of the legate). The legate was the commander of the whole legion.

2. *Principia.* This was the legion headquarters.

3. Houses of the six tribunes. One of the tribunes was second in command under the legate. The others had office jobs.

4. *Carcer* (prison).

5. Hospital.

6. *Schola* (education centre).

7. Granary.

8. Barracks where legionaries lived.

Siege!

The Roman army developed the art of capturing enemy cities by siege. The besieging army built siege towers, ramps and scaling ladders. A ramp leads up to a siege tower in the background of the picture. Soldiers can cross on to the city wall from the top of the tower. The tower is covered in skins to prevent it catching fire.

A *testudo* or "tortoise" of legionaries is advancing towards the gate on the right. The soldiers of the *testudo* carry their shields over their heads. This forms a shell of armour against enemy spears. There is a large catapult in the foreground. It could hurl rocks or flaming darts into the besieged city. The two walls and the ditch on the left have been built by the besieging army. They are to stop other armies from coming to help the people in the city.

Gods and sacrifices

Many people think that the Romans copied Greek religion and took over Greek gods and goddesses under different names. However, the Romans did not tell stories about the marriages and adventures of their gods. Roman gods were more like remote powers and less like ordinary men and women than Greek gods.

The Romans worshipped gods such as Jupiter, Mars and Apollo, and goddesses such as Juno, Minerva and Venus. The Romans also worshipped guardian spirits of the home called *Lares* and *Penates*. There was a shrine to the *Lares* and *Penates* in every household.

▶ This relief shows the Emperor Constantine (centre) celebrating a military victory. He will sacrifice a pig, a sheep and a bull to the gods. This ceremony was called the *Suovetaurilia* from the Latin words *sus* (pig), *ovis* (sheep) and *taurus* (bull). Notice the military standards, victory wreathes and the flute player.

◀ When a sick or wounded person had recovered his health, he gave a model of the healed part of the body to the gods in thanksgiving.

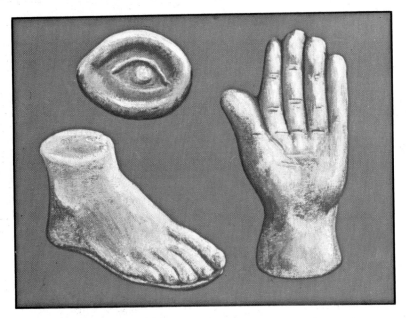

Every public event included sacrifices to the gods, but the chief worship took place in the temples. Each god had his or her own temple. Ordinary citizens could attend the temple services but they took little part in what went on. Priests and magistrates carried out the ceremonies according to ancient custom.

By the end of the Republican period, many Romans no longer believed so strongly in religion. Some of the temples were collapsing through neglect. People would still go to the temple to ask the god for a favour. They promised the god a present if the favour was granted. Religion was like a kind of exchange: "If you do something for me, I'll do something for you." Later it became the custom to worship the Emperor himself as a god.

▲ The Romans believed in magic. This model hand is marked with magic symbols to ward off the evil eye.

The story of Rome

753 BC This was the traditional date of the founding of Rome. For the first 250 years Rome was ruled by kings. After the last king, Tarquin the Proud, was deposed in 509 BC, Rome became a republic. Two consuls shared the power of the king. The citizens of Rome began to separate into two classes: the rich patricians and the poor plebeians.

As the city grew, the Romans protected their frontiers by conquering their nearest neighbours. Then they fought the tribes on their new frontiers. By 250 BC, they had conquered all Italy and were beginning to fight abroad. During this time, the Roman Law was written down as the Laws of the Twelve Tables, and the plebeians began a long struggle for equal rights with the patricians.

▲ The Romans fight to protect their frontiers.

146 BC Roman armies destroyed the city of Carthage. Rome had fought three wars against this rival republic. With Carthage destroyed, Rome increased her overseas possessions and became much more powerful. However, there was trouble in Rome itself. Riots broke out between the nobles and the common people. Rome had turned her war captives into slaves. In 73 BC, there was a huge slave revolt led by a gladiator called Spartacus. The revolt was cruelly put down by the Army.

▲ The gladiator, Spartacus, leads a slave revolt.

Roman politics were in chaos. Two powerful generals, Pompey and Julius Caesar, tried to control the government. After an early alliance Caesar and Pompey became enemies. Pompey was murdered and by 45 BC, Julius Caesar had become the sole ruler of Rome. The Senate plotted to kill him because they were afraid that he would make himself king.

44 BC Caesar was stabbed to death on March 15. His friend, Mark Antony, and his nephew, Octavian, fought and defeated the conspirators. In 33 BC Antony and Octavian quarrelled. Antony was defeated in battle. Octavian became head of the state and eventually the first Emperor, Augustus.

Augustus was a wise ruler. He began to develop a civil service to deal with the day-to-day running of the Empire; he gave important new jobs to freedmen and even to slaves. He was also popular with the people and improved the city by building new temples, libraries, theatres and public baths. Most important of all, he kept peace within the Empire.

▲ Julius Caesar is stabbed to death in the Senate.

AD 14 Augustus died in this year. He was succeeded by his stepson Tiberius, who was already 55 when he came to power. Tiberius was efficient but cruel. Any person that he suspected of treason was put to death. The last years of Tiberius's life were spent in retirement and the government of Rome gradually grew worse.

After the death of Tiberius, Caligula became Emperor. He ruled with such cruelty that people thought him mad. He was murdered by his own guards in AD 41. He was succeeded by his uncle, Claudius.

▲ The Emperor Claudius is poisoned by his wife.

AD 43 Claudius invaded Britain and added the southern part of the island to the Empire. Many large cities in the Empire had become important centres of commerce. They wanted more influence in the affairs of government. Claudius allowed a few of their important men to become Roman citizens.

Claudius was poisoned by his wife in AD 54, and her son, Nero, became Emperor. Nero is supposed to have played the lyre during a fire which destroyed most of Rome in AD 64. Nero was suspected of starting the fire himself, but he chose to blame the Christians and put many of them to death. Nero killed himself in AD 69. His death was followed by a period of chaos.

AD 161 Marcus Aurelius became Emperor. The Empire continued to grow until AD 180, but its best years were over. There were many changes of Emperor. Most of them were deposed or murdered by the army. By AD 252, barbarian tribes had begun to invade the Empire.

AD 337 The Emperor Constantine was baptized a Christian on his deathbed. After years of persecution, Christianity became the official religion of the Empire.

AD 410 The Goths sacked the city of Rome. The legions were recalled from Britain and the island was abandoned. In AD 455 Rome was sacked a second time by the Vandals.

AD 476 A Gothic chieftain called Odoacer deposed the last emperor in Rome and declared himself king of Italy. The Western Empire was destroyed. The Empire continued in the East, with the capital at Byzantium. In AD 1453 the Eastern Empire was overrun by the Ottoman Turks.

Fall of an empire

The Romans built an Empire almost without realizing it. They conquered their nearest neighbours in order to make their frontiers safe. Then they fought and defeated new enemies on new frontiers.

At first the Romans probably did not intend to build an Empire. They just did what seemed necessary at the time.

But what happened when the Empire began to crumble? Did the Romans know that their world was coming to an end? Everything seemed to be going on as usual. Roman soldiers still fought the wild tribes on the frontiers. The Senate still met in Rome. There were still shows to go to and processions to watch.

However, barbarian tribes were beginning to invade Roman territories without being driven back. The Emperor's guards tried to sell the position of Emperor to the highest bidder. There were civil wars. Emperors were murdered.

The Romans soon had to pay barbarian chiefs large sums of money to stop them attacking the frontiers. Ordinary citizens had to cover the cost of this by paying heavy taxes. Prices grew higher. The Empire was almost bankrupt. Outbreaks of plague and a severe famine made matters worse.

At the end of the third century AD, the Emperor, Diocletian, tried to stop the collapse by making two emperors, one to rule the East and one to rule the West. In AD 330, Constantine moved the Empire's capital from Rome to Byzantium. By AD 395, the Empire had broken into two separate states. The Eastern Empire remained strong and was to last for another thousand years.

Barbarians from the north swept into the Western Empire. The great city of Rome was destroyed. After 1200 years, nothing was left save a heap of ruins.

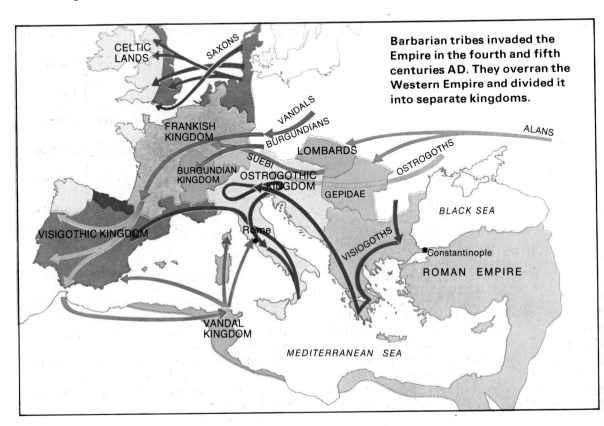

Barbarian tribes invaded the Empire in the fourth and fifth centuries AD. They overran the Western Empire and divided it into separate kingdoms.

The Roman influence

The Roman Empire in the West ceased to exist, but the influence of Ancient Rome is still felt strongly in the modern world, as it has been through the ages.

When Christianity became the official religion of Rome, the Catholic Church adopted Roman organization and tradition. After the collapse of Rome, the power of the Church spread all over Europe.

It took with it Roman ideas of order and the Latin language. The Church saved many books by Roman writers. These books found their way into monastery libraries. When schools and colleges were established, the pupils were taught Latin and they read books by Romans.

Lands that had once been Roman provinces became independent kingdoms. The invaders brought languages but Latin was not forgotten. The languages of the new kingdoms adopted many of the words of the old Roman world.

Roman architecture has always been copied. In various parts of the world, you can see arches, bridges, aqueducts, tunnels and domes which owe their shape to Roman influence. The towns of Canada and the US are built on a grid plan like the grid plan used by the Romans to build their towns.

We have also inherited Roman ideas about society and how people should live together. Some of these ideas came from the Greeks. The Romans added their own flair for organization and order. They were the first to make the Greek ideas work on a large scale.

Perhaps Rome's system of law and justice was her greatest legacy to the world. The Twelve Tables and the written law of the Emperor Justinian (The Justinian Code) still form the basis of Western law.

LATIN	Meaning	ITALIAN	FRENCH	ROMANIAN	SPANISH	ENGLISH
aqua (aquae)	water	acqua	eau	apă	agua	aquatic
lex (legis)	law	legge	loi	lege	ley	legal
civis (civis)	citizen	cittadino	citoyen	cetătean	ciudadano	citizen
communis (communis)	common	comune	commun	comun	común	common
populus (populi)	people	popolo	peuple	popor	pueblo	populace
nox (noctis)	night	notte	nuit	noapte	noche	nocturnal
sal (salis)	salt	sale	sel	sare	sal	saline
turris (turris)	tower	torre	tour	turn	torre	turret

The Latin language forms the basis of the Italian, Spanish, Portuguese, French, Catalan, Romanian, Romansh and Provençal languages. There are also many Latin words in the Dutch, Albanian, German and English languages.

In the chart above, there are some examples of words in modern European languages which come from Latin words. The word in brackets beside each Latin word is the genitive, or possessive, form. It is the Latin genitive that sometimes forms the basis of words in modern languages.

The Italian, French, Romanian and Spanish words have exactly the same meaning as the Latin. The English words have meanings very like the Latin meaning.

Famous Romans

Pompey (106-48 BC) was one of Rome's greatest generals. In 67 BC he was given three years to clear the Mediterranean of pirates. He did the job in three months. He campaigned in the Middle East and added Asia Minor to the Empire. Pompey ruled the Empire with Julius Caesar for a time, and he married Caesar's daughter. After her death in 54 BC, Pompey and Caesar became rivals for supreme power. Caesar defeated Pompey in battle in 48 BC. Pompey fled to Egypt where he was murdered.

Julius Caesar (100-44 BC) was a great soldier and politician. He conquered all the warrior tribes of Gaul and added Gaul to the Empire. He landed in Britain in 55 BC and again in 54 BC. He wrote a book about his experiences as a military commander. He became dictator of Rome. When it seemed likely that Caesar would declare himself king, his enemies decided to kill him. He was assassinated on the Ides of March, 44 BC.

Cicero (104-43 BC) was a famous orator. He was a trained lawyer and his fiery speeches in the Senate gained him great reputation and influence. One speech resulted in a group of conspirators being executed without trial. Afterwards, he was sent into exile. Later he made his peace with Caesar and returned to Rome. He was murdered by order of Mark Antony after Caesar's death.

Mark Antony (82-30 BC) was Caesar's friend and right hand man. After Caesar's death he ruled the Empire with Octavian. Antony fell in love with Queen Cleopatra of Egypt and left his wife, who was Octavian's sister. The two men had little in common and this worsened the breach between them. Octavian defeated Antony in battle and Antony and Cleopatra committed suicide.

Augustus (63 BC-AD 14) Octavian was Caesar's heir. After Caesar's death Octavian and Mark Antony ruled the Empire. After Antony's downfall, Octavian ruled alone. He became the first Roman Emperor and was known as Augustus which was a title rather like 'His Majesty'. He was an excellent administrator. He ruled the Empire wisely for 40 years.

Lucretius (96-52 BC) was a poet and philosopher. He wrote a long poem called *The Nature of the Universe*. This poem explained how the universe worked. It denied that the gods had any interest in the affairs of men. Lucretius's work was based on the work of Epicurus, a famous

The Emperor Hadrian

Greek philosopher. Lucretius is supposed to have died after drinking a poisoned love potion.

Vergil (70-19 BC) was a farmer's son and perhaps Rome's greatest poet. His early poetry, the *Bucolics*, shows his love for his native Italy. He was a shy man but he became very famous during his lifetime. His best known work was the *Aeneid*. This was the story of Aeneas the Trojan and the founding of Rome. Vergil died before finishing it. Before his death he asked his friends to burn the manuscript. The *Aeneid* was published, however, by order of the Emperor, Augustus.

Horace (65-8 BC) was the son of a freedman who became a taxgatherer and bought a small farm. He gave his son a Roman education. Horace's lands were confiscated after he had fought in battle against Antony and Octavian and he had to work as a secretary. Horace is best known for his four books of Odes.

Livy (59 BC-AD 17) wrote a history of Rome in 142 books. Only a part of this history has survived. The writing is brilliant but it is not very accurate history. Livy's work told the story of Rome from its beginnings until his own time. His writing was very patriotic and praised all things Roman.

Tacitus (AD 55-116) was a Roman historian. His two best known works, the Annals and the Histories, tell the story of Rome from the death of Augustus to the death of Domitian. Tacitus was deeply concerned with public morals. He did not like the early Emperors and accused them of many crimes.

Trajan (AD 53-117) was born in Spain. He became Emperor in AD 98. He was an able ruler and a fine soldier. He extended the Empire to its greatest size. Trajan improved the government of the Roman provinces and under his rule the Empire prospered. He established a welfare system for orphan children. He adopted as his son another Spaniard, Hadrian, who succeeded him as Emperor.

Hadrian (AD 76-138) became Emperor when Trajan died. He recalled troops from some of the more distant frontiers and reduced the size of the Empire. He spent much of his time touring the Empire and improving its defences. During a visit to Britain he built his famous wall across the country. He was interested in law and made sure that it was the same throughout the Empire.

The great orator, Cicero

The Roman Empire AD 117

Oceanus
Germanicus

Eburacum
York

BRITANNIA

Londinium

GERMANIA
INFERIOR

Oceanus Britannicus

Colonia Agrippina

BELGICA

Lutetia
Paris

Moguntiacum

Durocortorum

LUGDUNENSIS   GALLIA

Oceanus
Atlanticus

AQUITANIA   GERMANIA   RHAETIA
              SUPERIOR
                           NORICUM

Lugdunum

Burdigala   ALPES   Aquileia
Bordeaux   PANNO

TARRACONENSIS   Vienna   Mediolanum
                  NARBONENSIS   Sirm
                         Arelate   Bononia
Caesaraugusta   Massilia   *Bologna* Ravenna
LUSITANIA *Saragossa* Narbo-   ILLYRICU
Olisipo   Martius   Salona

HISPANIA   Tarraco   CORSICA   ITALIA

Emerita Augusta   Roma   Dyrrhac
                                         Herculaneum
Hispalis •Corduba   SARDINIA   Pompeii   Apo
Gades •BAETICA   Carthago Nova   Brundisiun
  •Tingis   Mare Internum

TINGITANA   Caesarea   SICILIA
                                    Hippo Regius
                         Bulla Regia •Carthago
MAURETANIA CAESARIENSIS Cirta•   Thugga   Syracusae
                         Thamugadi• *Dougga*
                         Timgad Sufetula
                                   Sbeitla

AFRICA   •Leptis Magna

This map shows the Roman Empire at its
greatest extent. When the Emperor Trajan died in AD 117, Rome's 43 provinces
occupied over five million square kilo-
metres (two million square miles). Trajan's successor, Hadrian, withdrew Roman
troops from Mesopotamia, Armenia and
Assyria. He strengthened the Empire's
defences and built fortifications along the
whole northern frontier.
The modern names for some of the towns
are in italics under the Latin names.

The position of the Roman Empire in the world.

DACIA
• Apulum
• Sarmizegethusa

MOESIA

THRACIA
Byzantium

CEDONIA
• Thessalonica

US
ACHAEA
• Athenae

• Corinthus
Sparta

CRETA

Mare Internum

Cyrene

CYRENAICA

AEGYPTUS

Memphis •

Alexandria •

Pontus Euxinus

• Sinope

BITHYNIA
PONTUS

• Nicomedia

CAPPADOCIA

ASIA

• Ancyra

• Caesarea

GALATIA   CILICIA

LYCIA   PAMPHYLIA

• Ephesus

• Tarsus

CYPRUS

ARMENIA

Mare Caspium

Nisibis •

MESOPOTAMIA

ASSYRIA

• Antiochia

Euphrates   *Tigris*

SYRIA   • Palmyra

• Damascus

Caesarea •   • Bostra

JUDAEA

Hierosolyma
Jerusalem

• Petra

ARABIA

0   400   800   km

0   300   600 miles

Sinus Arabicus

World history 800 BC to AD 500

Rome

Europe

Asia

	Rome	Europe	Asia
800 BC	Rome is founded by Romulus in about 753 BC. A city develops on the seven hills beside the River Tiber. The Romans are ruled by kings for 250 years. The last three kings are Etruscan.	The Etruscans invade Italy. By the sixth century BC they dominate a large part of the country. Celts settle in Britain and begin to trade with the Phoenicians. Greek colonies flourish along the northern shores of the Mediterranean.	Chinese law is written down. China becomes a federation o seven states. The doctrine of reincarnation is developed in India. Buddha is born in 519 E
500 BC	The last king, Tarquin the Proud, is deposed in 509 BC. Rome becomes a republic and joins the Latin League. She makes war with her neighbours and gradually conquers all Italy. Rome begins to fight Carthage in 264 BC. Carthage is destroyed in 146 BC.	There is war between Greece and Persia. The Greek states unite and defeat the Persians. Philip of Macedon forms Greece into a federation in 336 BC. Philip is succeeded on his death by his son Alexander.	Confucius teaches in China. Alexander of Macedon reach India, but turns back without conquering it.
100 BC	Roman armies conquer the neighbouring Mediterranean countries. Spartacus leads a slave revolt in 73 BC. The Romans invade Britain in 55 and 54 BC. Julius Caesar is assassinated in 44 BC. The Republic collapses and Augustus becomes Emperor.	The conquered peoples of Europe are ruled by Romans. Greece becomes a Roman province, but Athens is still a free city.	The Han dynasty reigns in Ch The teachings of Confucius a written down. Silk trade deve with the West and caravan routes are opened up to Persi and Rome.
AD 1	Augustus dies in AD 14. He is succeeded by his stepson, Tiberius. The Empire grows. Provincial cities demand a larger share in government. Roman citizenship is granted to important provincials. Rome is burned and Nero is suspected of starting the fire.	Celtic tribes flee from Roman Gaul and take refuge in Britain. Britain is conquered in AD 43. Two Emperors are appointed, one by the legions in Spain and one by the legions on the Rhine. There is civil war and disorder. This comes to an end when Vespasian becomes Emperor in AD 69.	In China, Wang Meng usurp the Han throne and attempts radical social reform. Bore h 610 metres (2,000 ft.) deep, are drilled in the salt mines of Szechwan. Indian Buddhists bring their doctrine to China The Chinese invent paper.
AD 100 / **AD 500**	Hadrian becomes Emperor in AD 117. He reduces the size of the Empire and improves its defences. Diocletian (AD 245-313) appoints two Emperors, one to rule the West and one the East. Constant war strains Roman resources. Rome is sacked by the Vandals in AD 455.	Barbarian tribes start attacking the frontiers of the Empire in northern Europe. The Goths cross the River Danube in AD 376 and settle inside the Empire. Gaul is invaded by barbarians. The Western Empire collapses. The Visigoths, Suevi and Vandals set up their own kingdoms.	A Taoist group, the "Yellow Turbans", revolt and cause t collapse of the Han dynasty. The unification of China is attempted by the Western C dynasty. The northern areas are abandoned to the barbar invaders.

frica	Near East	America	

			800 BC
pt is invaded by the rians and the city of Thebes cked. Egypt becomes pendent of Assyria. Egypt es with Greece.	Palestine is divided into Judah and Israel. Both peoples are conquered by the Assyrians, who in turn are overthrown by Medes and Babylonians. Persia becomes powerful.	Olmec peoples are powerful in Mexico. Their priest rulers build great temples. The Olmecs invent the calendar.	**500 BC**
on industry develops in the ite city of Meroe. The ians conquer and rule Egypt. Greeks help the Egyptians feat the Persians. ander builds Alexandria.	The Persian Empire grows. Persia tries to conquer Greece but is thrown back. Then Persia is conquered by Alexander of Macedon 150 years later.	The Mayas capture Monte Alban, city of the Olmecs and Zapotecs. The Jaguar religion and the custom of human sacrifice is established.	**100 BC**
Ptolemies rule as Pharaohs ypt. Cleopatra meets Julius ar, and later Mark Antony. ny is defeated at Actium ctavian (Augustus). The u peoples spread across ern and eastern Africa.	Greek culture and influence spread through the Near East. Rome conquers the whole area, including Palestine. Jesus is born at Nazareth.	The Paracas culture develops in Peru. They make beautiful textiles.	**AD 1**
t becomes part of the an Empire. Augustus forbids tors to visit Egypt without rmission.	The Jews rebel against the Romans in AD 66. The revolt is crushed.	Early Mayan settlers begin to build temples and pyramids. The Toltecs build the great city of Teotihuacan in Mexico.	**AD 100**
tianity begins to trickle gypt through its Jewish nunities. The first Christian rts are among the ucated masses of the e. Alexandrian Christianity ops in Egypt. Egyptian s are the first in endom.	The Jews are driven out of Jerusalem in AD 135. The Romans forbid them to return. Christianity spreads throughout the eastern provinces of the Roman Empire. Christians are persecuted until the Emperor Constantine is converted to Christianity in AD 337.	Hieroglyphics are used by the Mayas. The volcano Xitli erupts in AD 300 and buries the Cuicuilco pyramid in Mexico. Mayan civilization develops as a federation of city-states in Mexico, Guatemala and Honduras.	**AD 500**

Glossary

amphitheatre a large oval or circular building, with seats for spectators.

aqueduct a man-made channel for carrying water; often made of stone and raised above the ground.

archaeologist someone who studies historical remains.

dictator a ruler who had complete and absolute power in an emergency.

excavation the work of uncovering or digging up historical remains.

forum an open, public place.

fresco a wall painting.

fuller someone who cleaned cloth.

fuller's earth a kind of alkaline clay used by fullers to wash cloth.

grammaticus a teacher of Greek and Latin grammar, history, geography and astronomy.

ides a date of the Roman calendar. The ides were the 15th of March, May, July and October and the 13th of other months.

insula (plural: *insulae*) an island.

lar (plural: *lares*) a household god.

lararium shrine of the *lares*.

mosaic picture made up of small pieces, usually stone.

patrician a noble.

peristyle a covered passage around an open courtyard.

plebeian an ordinary working person.

podium a raised platform round the arena of an amphitheatre.

reconstruction an attempt to recreate something as it was in the past. A reconstruction can be a model, a painting, a building or an object.

relief a carving in which the figures or objects are slightly raised from a flat surface.

silphium a vegetable, now extinct.

testudo means tortoise-shell in Latin. The word was used to describe a method of attack in which soldiers advanced together with their overlapping shields held above them for protection.

tufa a kind of volcanic rock.

vomitoria passages for entrance and exit in an amphitheatre.

Index